Reptiles
Up Close

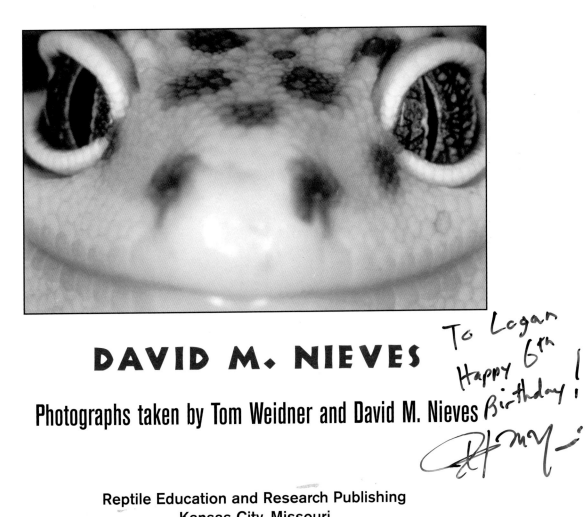

DAVID M. NIEVES

To Logan Happy 6th Birthday!

Photographs taken by Tom Weidner and David M. Nieves

Reptile Education and Research Publishing
Kansas City, Missouri

Book cover and interior design by Tim Lynch
Book publishing services by BookWorks Publishing, Marketing, Consulting
All photographs taken by Tom Weidner and David M. Nieves

Publisher's Cataloging-in-Publication
Nieves, David M.
    Reptiles up close / David M. Nieves - 1st ed.
    p. cm.
    Includes bibliographical references.
    SUMMARY: Explores eleven species of reptiles, including snakes, geckos, crocodiles, Gila monsters, and turtles, with close-up photographs and questions to ponder.
    LCCN: 99-91034
    ISBN: 978-0-9673958-0-7

      1. Reptiles-Pictorial works-Juvenile literature.
    I. Title.

QL644.2.N54 1999   597.9
                QBI99-1294

Dedication

To my parents, Roland and Marta, who taught me compassion, perseverance, and the value of hard work. They also taught me to dream and set goals.

To my love, Michelle, and our three beautiful daughters: Ciara, Savannah, and Mia. I never realized what I was missing in my life until you entered it. Now I can't imagine it without you.

2

Acknowledgments

I would like to thank Tom Weidner, a kind, generous, and trusted friend, for taking time out of his busy schedule to be a part of this project. His herpetological and photographic experience was invaluable in creating this book.

Thanks also to Jeff Ettling and Norman Haskell for digging through their respective libraries to find obscure Latin translations. Special thanks to Linda Weidner, David Tompkins, Terry L. Vandeventer, and David Van Den Baard for assisting during the photography sessions.

Table of Contents

Introduction

Scientists have discovered over 8,000 different species of reptiles worldwide. This includes about 4,800 lizards, 2,900 snakes, 300 turtles and tortoises, 23 crocodilians, and 2 tuataras. More species are still being discovered and named. Reptiles come in many shapes, sizes, colors, and patterns. They live all over the world except for the North Pole and South Pole, where it is too cold. Their habitats include the ocean, deserts, woodlands, marshes, rainforests, and just about everything in between.

Reptiles are hard to study. Most reptiles are shy and secretive. They spend most of their time hiding, like this Banded Rock Rattlesnake. They aren't hiding so they can jump out and get you. They are hiding because they don't want you to find them. Did you ever have a day where you wanted to be left alone? Almost every day is like that for reptiles.

This book is full of "up close" pictures of different reptiles. A special camera was used to take these photos. Do not try to get this close to a live reptile and never stick your face in a reptile's face.
If you get too close to a reptile, it might become scared and bite to defend itself.

There are 11 species of reptile in this book. For each one, you will first see four extreme close-up pictures. Then you will see a picture of the whole reptile in a natural environment. Try to figure out where each close-up picture fits on the reptile. Sometimes the picture is easy, like this Dwarf Crocodile's back foot (A). Sometimes the picture is hard, like the top of a Dwarf Crocodile's head (B).

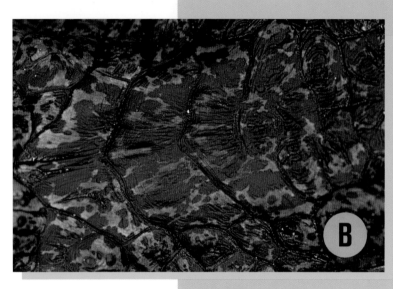

You will also find fun information about each species. Scientists give every animal a special scientific name in the ancient languages of Latin or Greek. For each reptile in this book, the scientific name is explained. Each chapter ends with an "Explore More" question. Some "Explore More" questions will need your imagination, for others you may need to look up the answers. If you need help finding the answers, ask a parent, a teacher, or a librarian.

Now, turn the page and enjoy looking at, and learning about, some incredible reptiles.

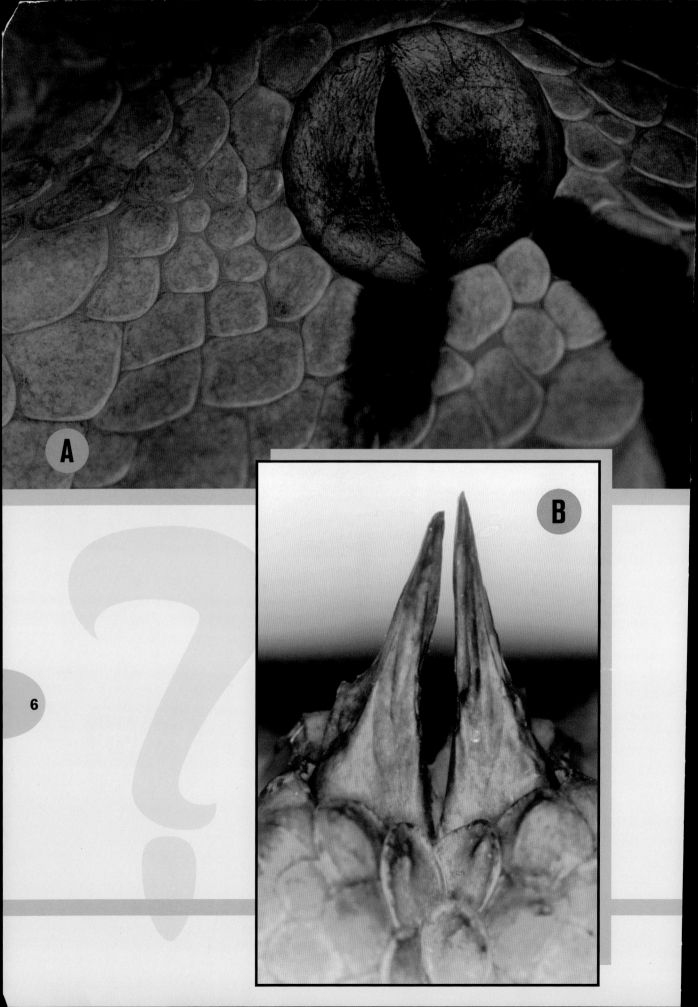

A

B

6

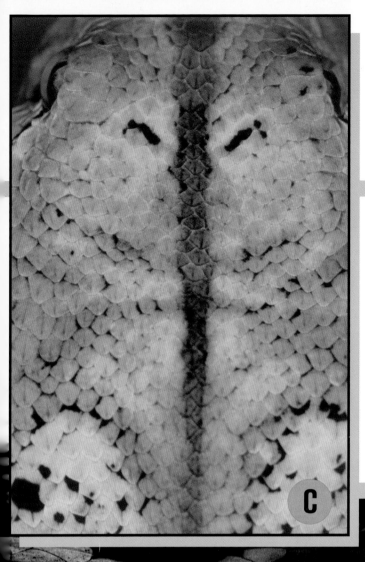

C

What is it?

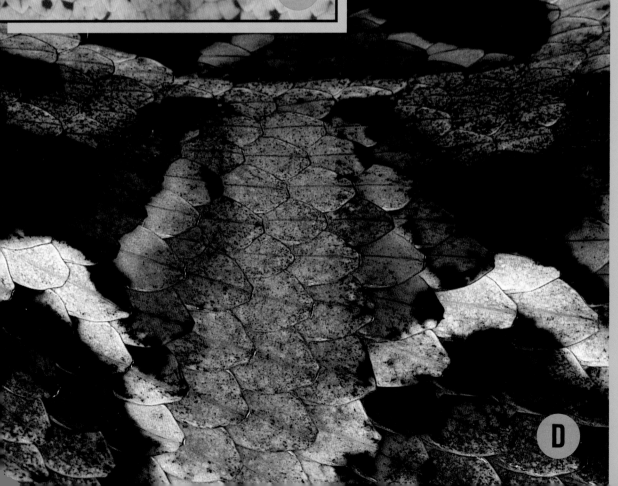

D

7

Gaboon Viper

Scientific Name: *Bitis gabonica*

Translation of scientific name:

"bitis = to bite, gabonica = from Gabon area of Africa"

Answers:

A. The eye

B. The horns on the nose

C. The top of the head

D. The side of the snake's body

This large snake has beautiful camouflage. An adult Gaboon Viper can be six feet long and almost one foot wide in the middle. It is venomous and lives on the forest floor of Central Africa. This snake has very long fangs, sometimes up to two inches in a very large Gaboon Viper. These special front teeth fold up when the mouth is closed, so the snake doesn't accidentally bite itself.

Snakes shed their teeth every few months and have new teeth ready to replace the old, lost ones. The teeth that fall out usually end up being swallowed. Here is a picture of some of the fangs this snake has shed. They were found in the snake's poop. Can you imagine swallowing big fangs like these? Can you imagine them coming out the other end?

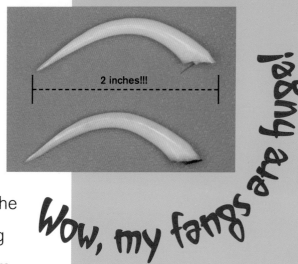

2 inches!!!

Wow, my fangs are huge!

The Gaboon Viper is very shy and uses its camouflage to hide in the leaves on the rainforest floor. There it waits for birds or small mammals to come close enough to eat. The two horns above its nose are soft, so it doesn't use them to poke at anyone. Instead, a Gaboon Viper's horns help make its head resemble a large dead leaf. The horns still help the Gaboon Viper defend itself, since they help it hide. What if you had two soft horns sticking up from your nose? They might get in the way when you put glasses on.

9

Explore More

The Gaboon Viper's horns help it camouflage. Can you name four other ways horns might help an animal?

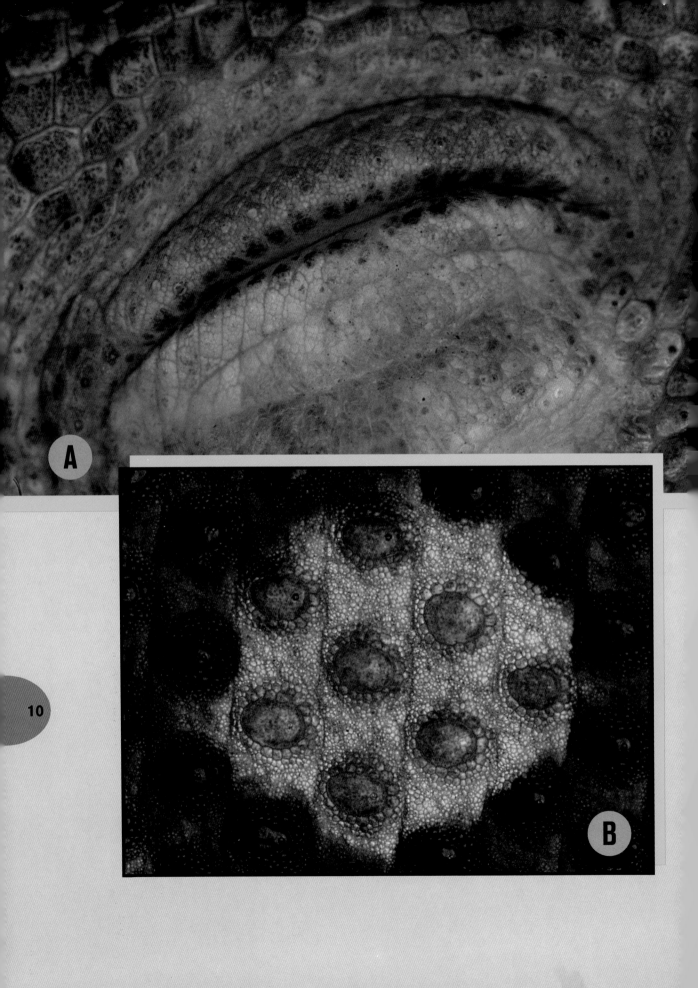

A

B

10

What is it?

C

D

Cape Monitor

Scientific Name: *Varanus albigularus*

Translation of scientific name:

"Varanus = warner or watcher, albigularus = white throat"

This large lizard is a powerful creature that can reach over six feet in length. It has strong legs, large claws, and a large muscular tail, which makes this lizard a great climber and digger. The Cape Monitor is found in grasslands and rocky habitats of Southern Africa where it hunts during the day. Animals that sleep at night and come out during the day are called "diurnal."

A Cape Monitor will eat any small animal that fits in its mouth. Large insects, land snails, rodents, birds, and other reptiles can all be on the menu. This lizard will even eat venomous snakes such as Cobras! However, the Cape Monitor has to watch out for bigger predators like lions, leopards, and hyenas, which might eat it.

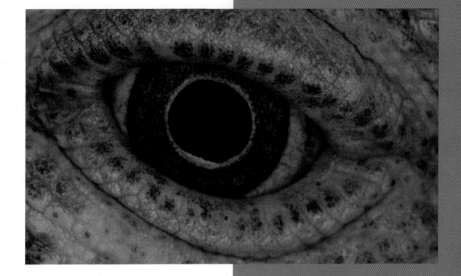

Behind this lizard's eye is a large hole on the side of its head. This is an ear. Lizards have ears but no big floppy earlobes sticking out like ours. Imagine what you would look like without big floppy earlobes sticking out of the side of your head. What would a lizard look like if it had big floppy earlobes?

Right in front of the Cape Monitor's eye is the hole for its nostril. The nostrils point right towards its eyes. Imagine if your nose was on your forehead and your nostrils pointed at your eyes. Sneezing would be quite messy.

I have to keep an eye out for any critter that fits in my mouth.

Explore More **Pick several animals with unusual ears or earlobes. Now imagine what it would be like to have ears or earlobes like theirs.**

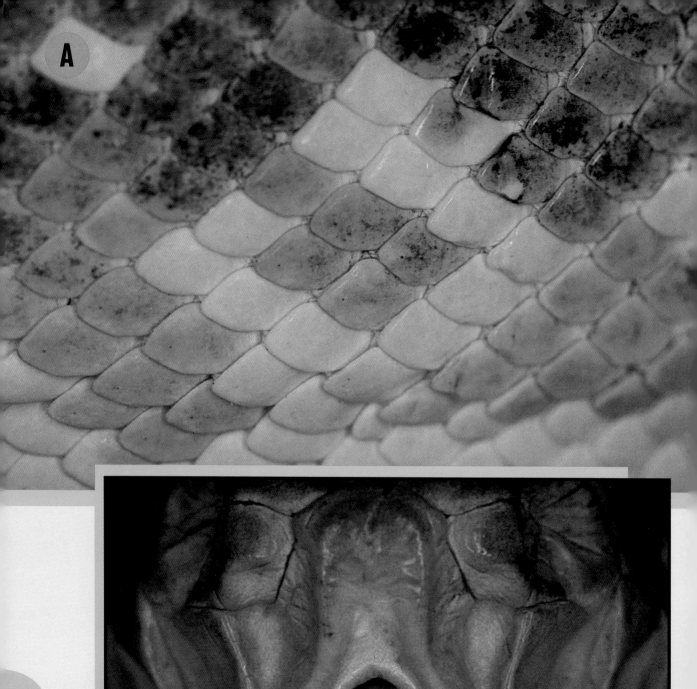

What is it?

C

D

Emerald Tree Boa

Scientific Name: *Corallus caninus*

Translation of scientific name:

"Corallus = shiny or pretty-colored, caninus = large front teeth"

Answers:

A. The Boa's lower side
B. The front of its face
C. A spot on its side
D. The eye

This bright green snake lives in South America's Amazon rainforest spending most of its life up in the trees. The Emerald Tree Boa has a strong tail that can wrap around a branch and support its entire weight. This is called a "prehensile" tail. Some monkeys have the same type of tail to help them climb. It might be fun to have a prehensile tail to help us climb better.

The Emerald Tree Boa can curl up its six-foot long body on a branch and camouflage itself as a clump of leaves. If it is thirsty it will drink morning dew off of leaves or rainwater off its back. Could you stand under a sprinkler and drink water off of your back?

The Emerald Tree Boa has several extra long front teeth. These teeth are twice as long as the rest of its teeth.

The top of my head is just as green as the rest of me.

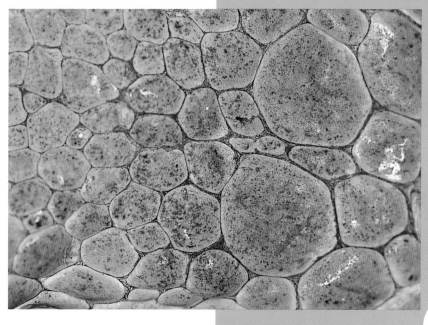

This snake will eat rodents and birds found in the trees. When the Emerald Tree Boa bites its prey, the special front teeth make sure dinner doesn't escape. Imagine having front teeth twice as long as the rest of your teeth.

There are over 30 species in the Boa family. Most Boas are small or medium-sized snakes like the Emerald Tree Boa. They live in many different types of habitats. Some Boa species can even live in the desert.

17

Explore More **Can you find the names of the two species of Boa that live in North America?**

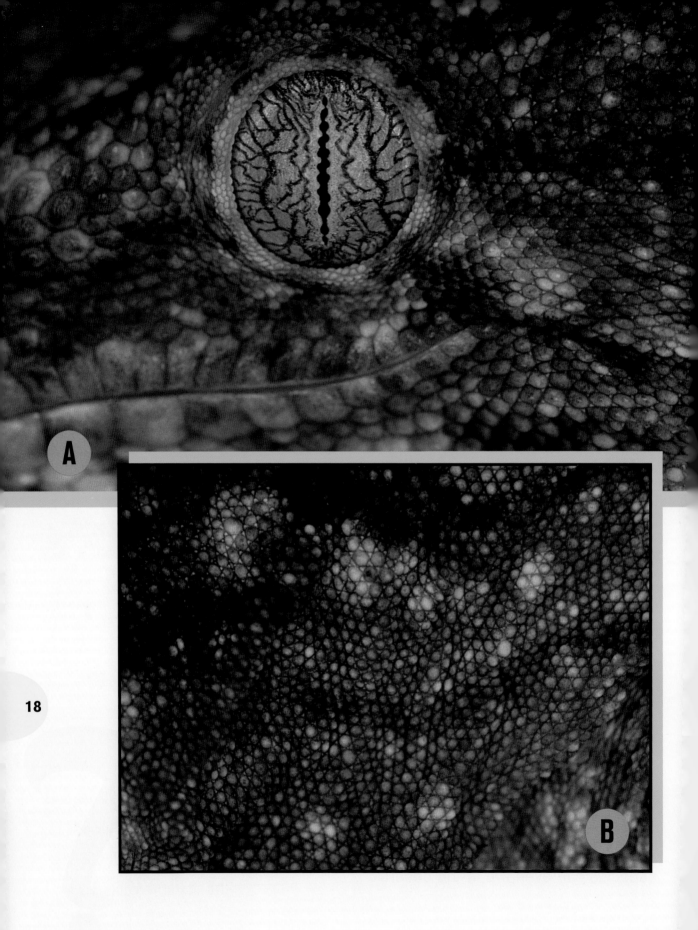

What is it?

C

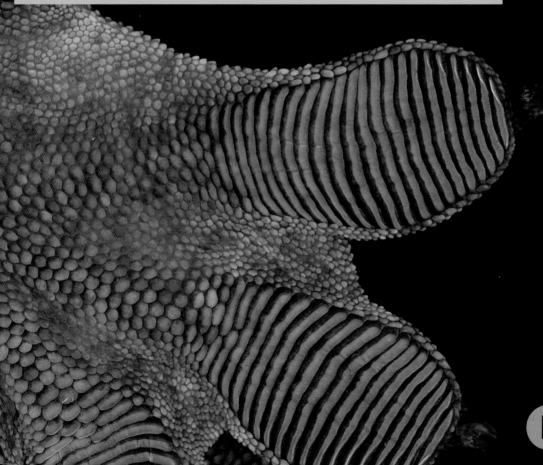

D

19

New Caledonian Giant Gecko

Scientific Name: *Rhacodactylus leachianus*

Translation of scientific name:

"Rhacodactylus = web-fingered, leachianus = named after William E. Leach"

Answers:

A. The eye

B. The Gecko's back

C. The top of the foot

D. The lamelle on the bottom of the feet

This lizard has incredible camouflage and is found on the Island of New Caledonia in the Pacific Ocean where it lives in the forests high up in the trees. There are over 800 species of lizards in the Gecko family. The New Caledonian Giant Gecko can grow to over 12 inches long, making it one of the largest Gecko species. It will sleep all day and then come out at night looking for food, which

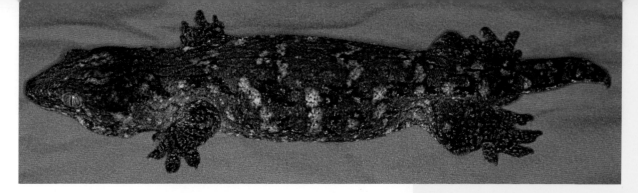

means it is "nocturnal." A big part of its diet is fruit found in the trees. But the New Caledonian Giant Gecko will also eat insects, spiders, other lizards, and small birds. Eating both plants and animals makes it an "omnivore."

The New Caledonian Giant Gecko is an excellent climber due to special pads on its toes called "lamellae." The lamellae are covered with thousands of tiny, microscopic hairs called "setae." These setae can stick to almost any surface, allowing the New Caledonian Giant Gecko to walk across a ceiling or climb up glass. This lizard can even control when the setae grip and when they let go. If it couldn't, the New Caledonian Giant Gecko would never be able to let go of anything. It would be permanently stuck to everything it touched.

This lizard's tail is short, but very strong and prehensile like the Emerald Tree Boa's. The New Caledonia Giant Gecko even has lamellae at the end of its tail to help it climb better. Most other Geckos don't have tails like this.

Can you see me now?

Explore More **Think of ways lamellae would help you besides making you a better climber.**

21

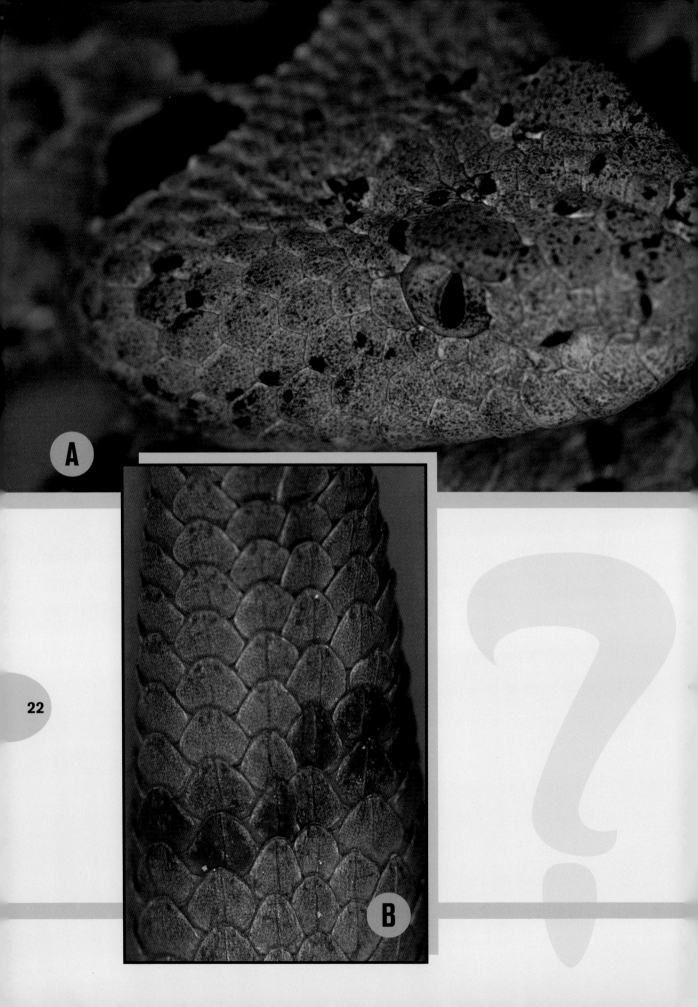

A

B

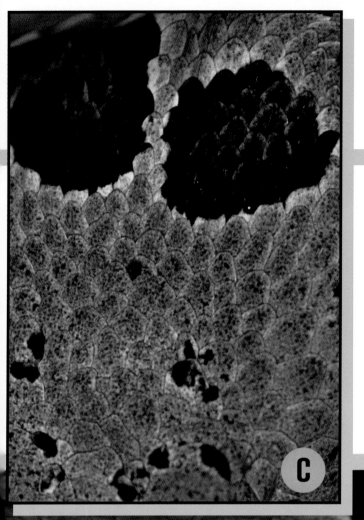

C

What is it?

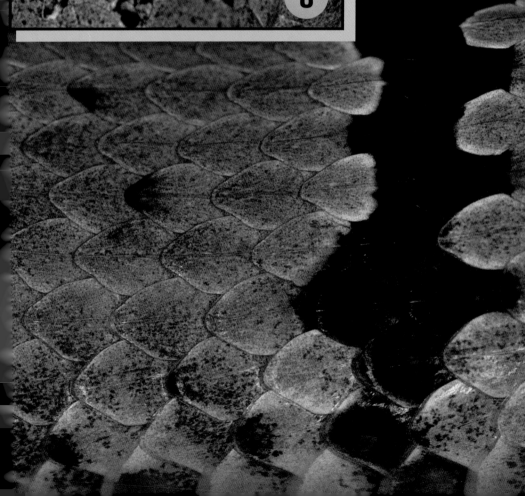

D

Banded Rock Rattlesnake

Scientific Name: *Crotalus lepidus*

Translation of scientific name:

"Crotalus = rattle, lepidus = pleasant"

Answers:

A. The eye

B. The end of the tail

C. The top of the head

D. One of the snake's black bands

This beautiful, small species of Rattlesnake is usually less than three feet long. The Banded Rock Rattlesnake is found in Arizona and New Mexico in the Southwestern United States where it lives in rocky hill habitats. Even though it is small, it is still dangerous. Venomous snakes should always be left alone.

A Rattlesnake uses its venom for defending itself

and for killing its prey. The Banded Rock Rattlesnake eats lizards and mice. The snake's slender body lets it follow mice down into holes. Since mice can cause a lot of problems for people, snakes are doing us a favor by eating them.

The Banded Rock Rattlesnake is amazing. It has an incredible rattle that can be shaken to make noise when it feels threatened. It isn't rattling to challenge you to a fight. The Rattlesnake is giving a

loud clear warning that tells you to back off and leave it alone. Leaving the Banded Rock Rattlesnake alone is the safest and smartest thing to do. Most people bitten by Rattlesnakes are bitten when they try to catch or hurt the snake.

The rattle at the tip of its tail is made out of the same stuff your fingernails are made of. It is called "keratin." Imagine having rattles on your fingertips. The rattle has several small parts, which fit loosely over each other. When the tail vibrates, the parts shake against each other and make the rattling noise. There are no sand or pebbles inside making the noise.

Just because I'm shaking my rattle,

doesn't mean I want to do battle.

25

What sounds do other animals make to warn us to leave them alone?

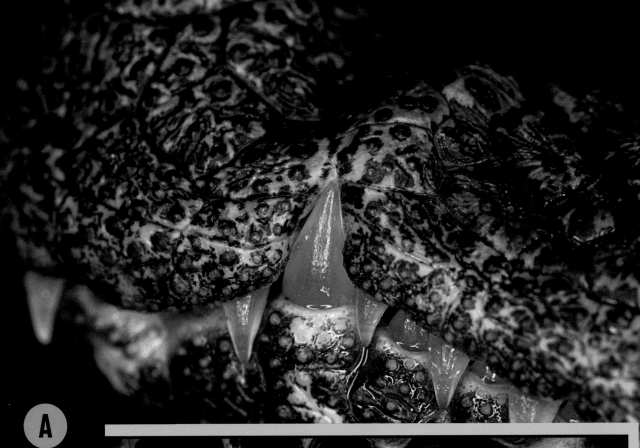

A

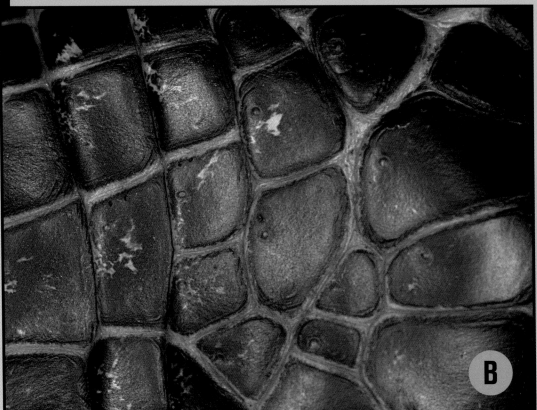

B

26

What is it?

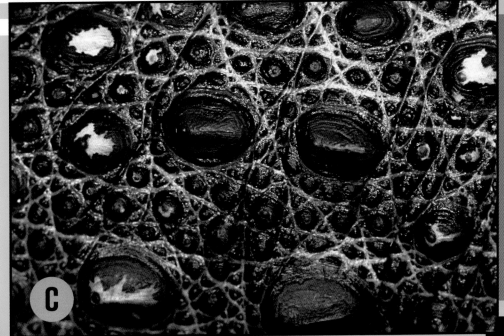

C

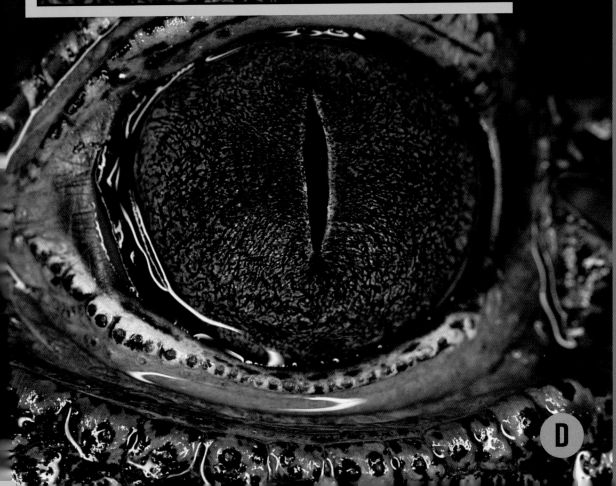

D

27

African Dwarf Crocodile

Scientific Name: *Osteolaemus tetraspis*

Translation of scientific name:

"Osteolaemus = bony throat, tetraspis = four shields "

28

Answers:

A. The teeth

B. The scales on its chest

C. The scales on its side

D. The eye

The African Dwarf Crocodile is one of the smallest of the crocodilians. Usually less than six feet long when fully grown, it is found in the rivers and swamps of the central African rainforest. Sometimes it digs holes on land to sleep in. The Dwarf Crocodile is a carnivore and eats any small animal it can catch. This includes everything from crabs, snails, and fish to birds, mammals, and other reptiles.

One of the ways you can tell this is a crocodile, and not an alligator, is by looking at its teeth. The fourth tooth of the lower jaw sticks out and can be seen while the mouth is closed. All crocodiles have that same tooth sticking out. On the other hand, when an alligator's mouth is closed, the only teeth that you see sticking out are from the upper jaw.

I may be small but I'm still a crocodile.

Check out my fourth tooth.

The Dwarf Crocodile has excellent eyesight, which helps it see in the dark and under water. It also has three eyelids for each eye. First, a top and bottom one like ours. Then there is a third eyelid that comes out from the side. It is clear so the Dwarf Crocodile can see through it. The extra eyelid works like a pair of swim goggles to protect the eye under water.

The Dwarf Crocodile's scales feel like hard rubber. A crocodile's scales and skin won't get wrinkled like our skin does after a long bath. Since it might spend several days at a time in the water, a crocodile needs special scales and skin.

29

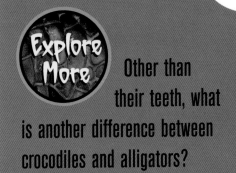

Explore More Other than their teeth, what is another difference between crocodiles and alligators?

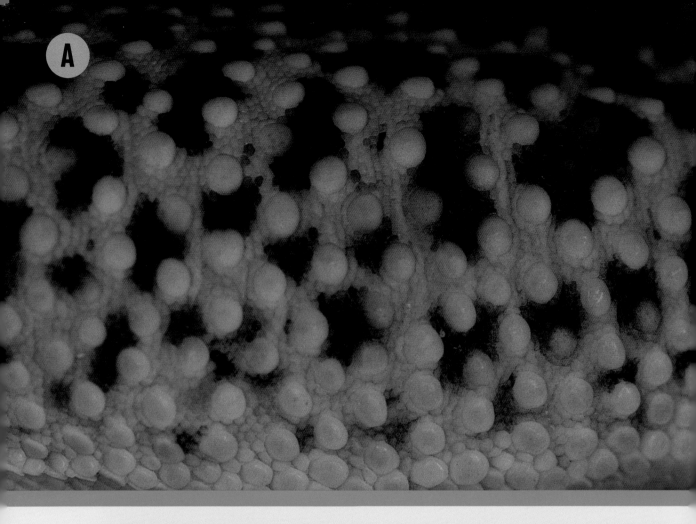

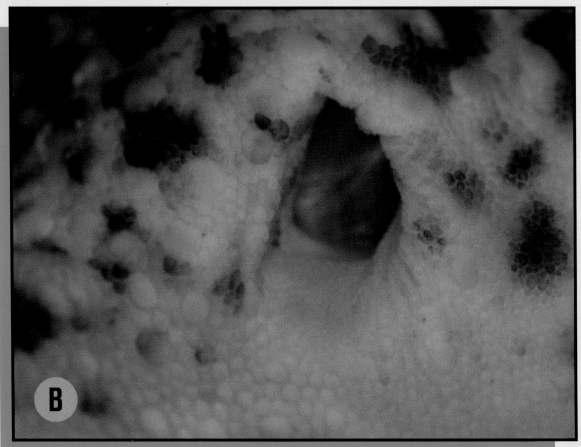

What is it?

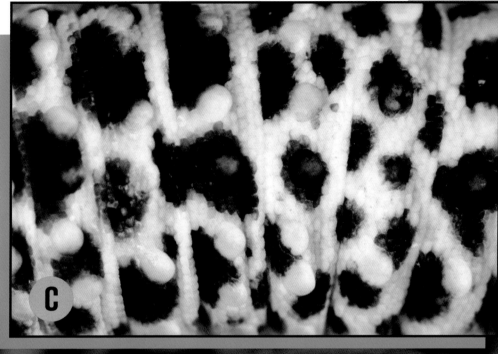

C

D

Leopard Gecko

Scientific Name: *Eublepharis macularius*

Translation of scientific name:

"*Eublepharis* = true eyelids, *macularius* = spotted"

Answers:

A. The side of its body
B. The Gecko's ear
C. The top of its tail
D. The eye

The Leopard Gecko is a small lizard that grows to about 11 inches long. It lives in rocky desert habitats of Pakistan and Afghanistan. The Leopard Gecko will get sick if it gets too hot, so this nocturnal lizard sleeps all day under a rock or deep in a hole. At night, when it is dark and cool, the Leopard Gecko hunts for food using its large eyes that can see in the dark. The Leopard Gecko eats insects, spiders, small mice, and even other smaller lizards.

Sometimes, while it crawls around on the ground, dirt or sand gets kicked up into its eyes. Instead of crying to wash them out, like we would do, the Leopard Gecko sticks out its long, flat, pink tongue and licks its eyes clean. If your tongue were long enough, do you think you would lick your eyes?

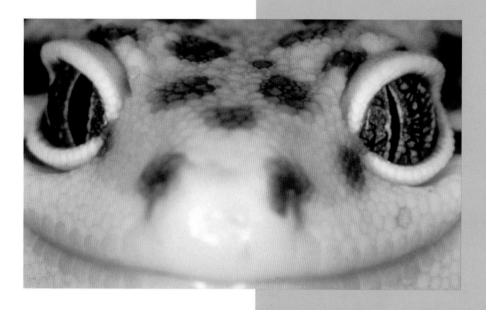

The Leopard Gecko's wide tail helps it to survive. The tail is full of fat, which acts like food and water when it can't find anything to eat. This is helpful in the desert where there isn't much food and water. The Leopard Gecko can survive several months without eating or drinking. During that time, its tail becomes very thin. When it finally finds food, the tail becomes wide again.

33

Explore More One reason the Leopard Gecko is nocturnal is to avoid the heat. What are two other reasons an animal might be nocturnal?

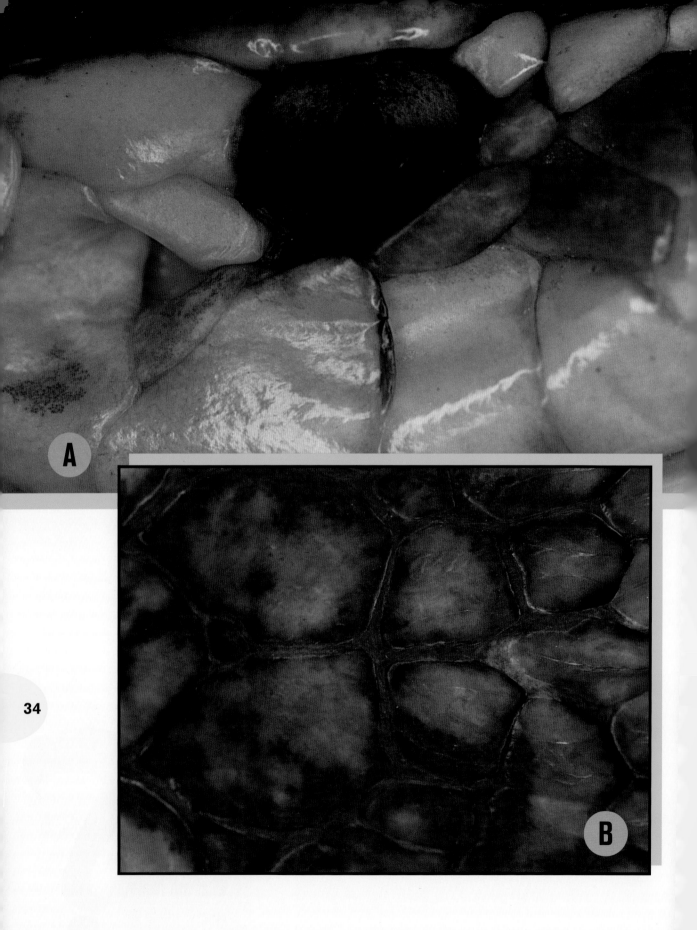

34

What is it?

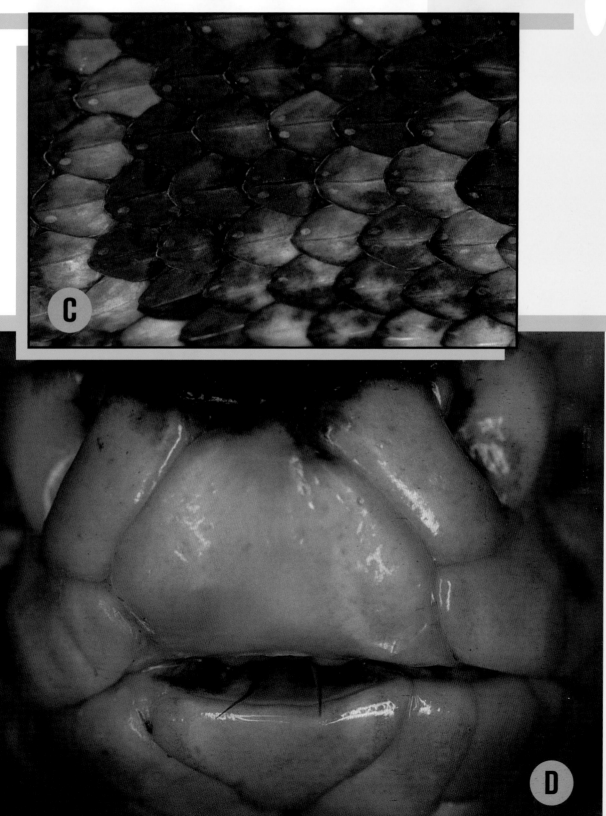

C

D

Cottonmouth

Scientific Name: *Agkistrodon piscivorus*

Translation of scientific name:

"Agkistrodon = hook toothed, piscivorus = fish-eater"

Answers:

A. The eye
B. The top of its head
C. The side of its body
D. The snake's mouth

The Cottonmouth is a venomous snake related to Rattlesnakes. It is sometimes called the Water Moccasin. The inside of its mouth is white and when this snake feels threatened, it will sometimes hold its mouth open as a warning. This is where the name Cottonmouth came from. This warning should never be ignored, since this snake's bite is very dangerous. But if you leave the Cottonmouth alone, it will leave you alone.

The Cottonmouth lives in swamps and marshes of the Southeastern United States where it feeds on fish, frogs, mice, rats, birds, turtles, and other snakes. A baby Cottonmouth's tail has a bright yellow tip, which can be wiggled back and forth like a worm to attract frogs. When a frog gets close enough the baby snake bites and eats the frog. Scientists call the yellow tail tip a "caudal lure." "Caudal" means tail and "lure" means to attract. It is kind of like fishing for frogs. Imagine fishing using part of your body as bait. When the baby snake grows up, its tail turns brown and black like the rest of its body. An adult Cottonmouth will go out and hunt for its food so it doesn't need a caudal lure anymore.

When I grow up, no more using my tail to get dinner.

The Cottonmouth is an excellent swimmer usually found in or around the water. Some people think every snake in the water is a Cottonmouth, but that is not true. There are many nonvenomous species of snake that live in or around the water in the United States. Several of them resemble the Cottonmouth. Books called *Field Guides* are excellent ways to learn how to identify reptiles that live in your area. Since all snakes have teeth and can bite to defend themselves it is best to identify them only by looking, not by grabbing or hurting them.

Explore More Can you find two other creatures that use part of their body to attract food?

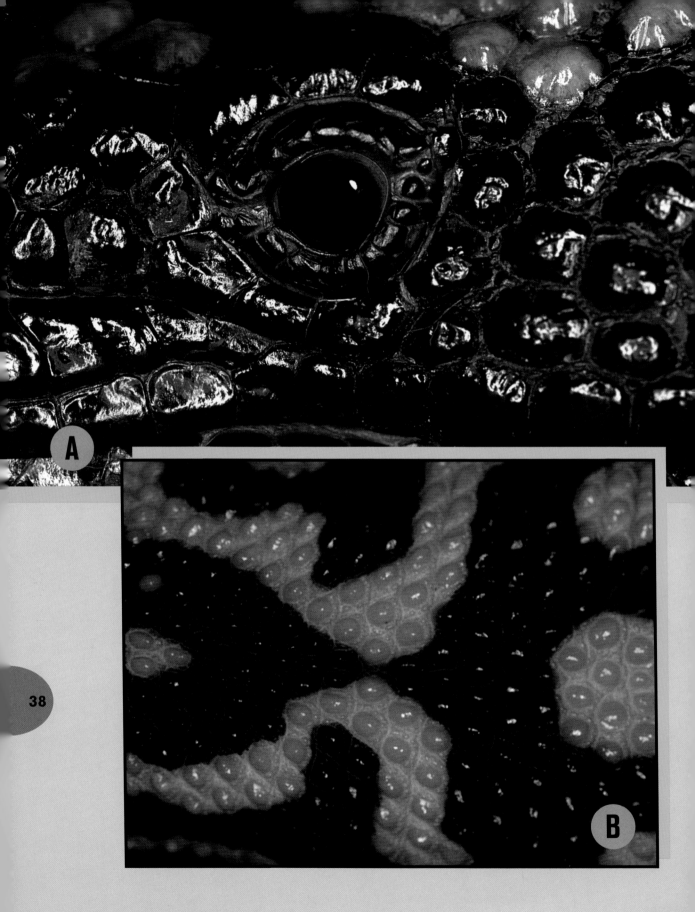

What is it?

C

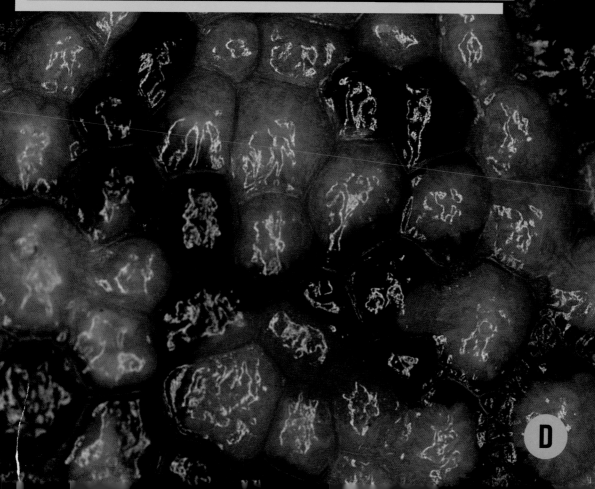

D

Gila Monster

Scientific Name: *Heloderma suspectum*

Translation of scientific name:

"Heloderma = studded skin, suspectum = suspicious"

Answers:

A. The eye

B. The scales on the back

C. The toes on its front foot

D. The scales on top of its head

The Gila Monster has an unusual name. It isn't really a monster, just a very colorful lizard. The bright colors are a warning to predators that this lizard has a dangerous, venomous bite. The Gila Monster and the Beaded Lizard are the only two species of venomous lizard. The Gila Monster is found in rocky desert habitats of the Southwestern United States and Northwestern Mexico.

The venom of the Gila Monster is used for defense and if a predator ignores the warning, this lizard will bite. Its venom causes intense pain and tremendous swelling. Any predator (or person) bitten by it will never forget the experience and won't make the same mistake again. When scientists first discovered the Gila Monster, they weren't sure if it was really venomous. That is why part of the scientific name means "suspicious."

The Gila Monster hunts at night and looks for rodent and bird nests on the ground. It will eat the young rodents and birds found in those nests. The Gila Monster's large tail can store fat like the Leopard Gecko's tail. The scales on the Gila Monster's stomach are flat, but the scales on its sides and back are bumpy and round. The flat stomach scales help the lizard slide over rocks that it climbs on. Reptiles usually have smoother scales on their stomachs.

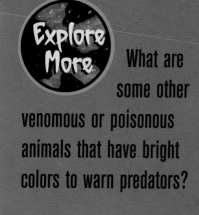

Explore More   What are some other venomous or poisonous animals that have bright colors to warn predators?

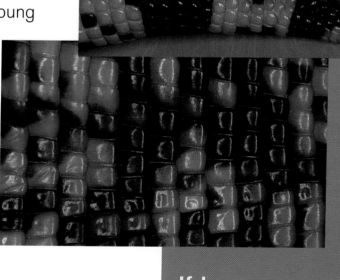

41

If I were a real monster, I would be knocking over buildings and starring in movies.

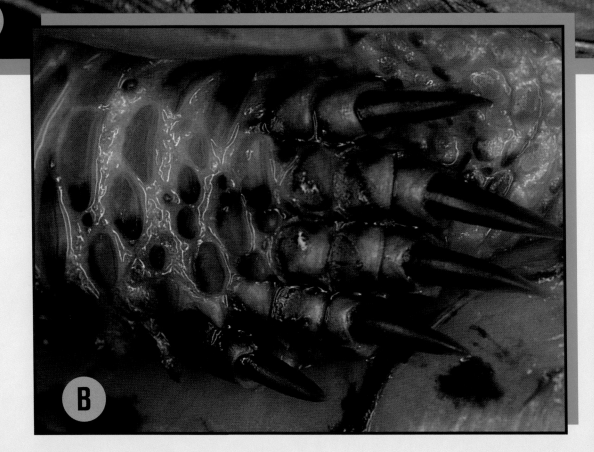

A

42

B

What is it?

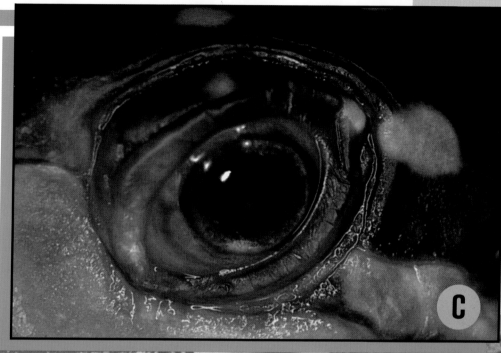

C

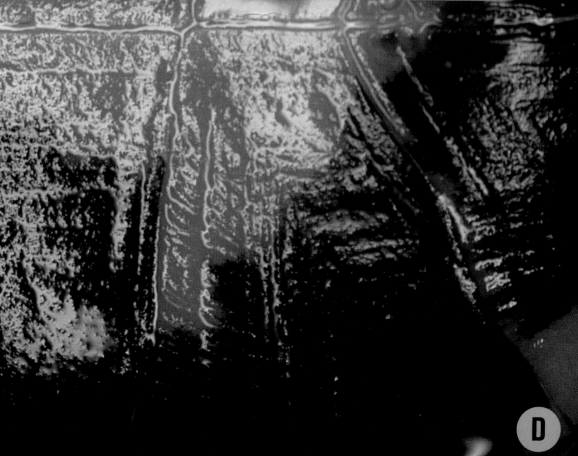

D

Spotted Turtle

Scientific Name: *Clemmys guttata*

Translation of scientific name:

"Clemmys = turtle, guttata = spotted"

Answers:

A. A spot on its shell

B. The front foot

C. The eye

D. The bottom of the shell

The Spotted Turtle lives in and around ponds or marshes of the Northeastern United States. Ponds and marshes are also known as wetlands. The Spotted Turtle is small, usually less than five inches long. It eats insects, worms, fish, tadpoles, and some plants. Like all turtles, it has a sharp beak, strong jaw muscles, and no teeth. Instead of chewing its food, the Spotted Turtle takes big bites and gulps them down. Maybe if we ate worms and tadpoles, we wouldn't chew either.

Because the Spotted Turtle lives both in water and on land, it swims and runs very well. If a predator is quick enough to catch it, the turtle pulls its head and legs into its shell for protection. Most predators get frustrated and leave the Spotted Turtle alone. Wouldn't it be fun to be

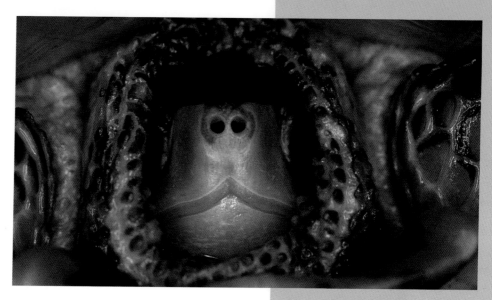

able to tuck your head into your shoulders if someone was bugging you?

The Spotted Turtle has become rare because of habitat destruction. Many wetlands have been drained or contaminated with chemicals. We can help the Spotted Turtle by learning how to protect and preserve wetlands.

Explore More What are some other animals that lose their home when a wetland is drained?

What is it?

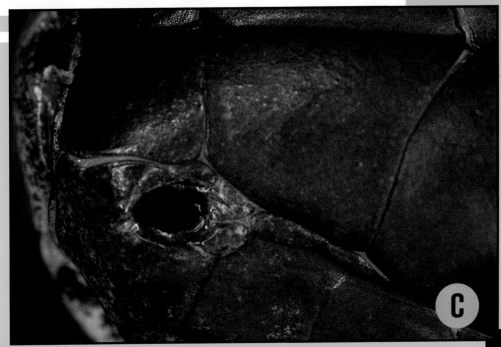

C

D

Short Python

Scientific Name: *Python brongersmai*

Translation of scientific name:

"Python = snake, *brongersmai* = named after Leo Brongersma".

This very strong snake is found in the rainforest of Indonesia. It can grow to about six feet long and has powerful muscles in its thick body. The Short Python hides in dead leaves on the forest floor where it waits for small mammals or birds to come close enough to eat. Imagine sitting in the middle of a kitchen and waiting for food to come close to your mouth.

Answers:

A. The eye

B. The scales on top of its head

C. The nostril

D. The side of its body

On the front of its face it has six small indentations called heat pits, which let the Short Python sense heat. Since the Short Python feeds on warm-blooded animals like birds and mammals, the heat pits let it know exactly where to strike so it doesn't miss. If the Short Python misses and the food escapes, it might have to wait weeks for another chance. Most other snakes don't have such pits.

Although it would rather eat every week, the Short Python can survive several weeks between meals. When it does eat, the Short Python can easily swallow one third of its own body weight. That is like a 150-pound person eating 50 pounds of food, which would be about 200 burgers. If you ate that much, maybe you could go a long time between meals too. After eating a big meal, sometimes the Short Python may not poop for two weeks. Do you think you could wait two weeks before the next time you go to the bathroom?

Here are three of my heat pits. With them I can sense warm things LIKE YOU!

49

Explore More

There are more than 20 species of Pythons. The world's smallest Python species lives in Australia. What is it called?

Reptiles as Pets

Reptiles have become very popular pets. Unfortunately, most of them don't make good pets. For example, many turtles need special diets to stay healthy and are very messy. Some lizards and snakes need huge, expensive cages to be comfortable. Crocodiles and alligators grow very large and become dangerous. Unlike dogs and cats, reptiles do not like to be cuddled, played with, or taken to the park for a walk.

However, caring for a reptile and studying its behavior can be very rewarding. People interested in owning a reptile need to learn how to care for it. Find out how long it lives, how big it grows, what and how often it eats, how much it poops, and what kind of cage it needs when full grown. Taking care of any animal is a big responsibility, so it is important to have a parent involved in choosing one.

There are many books available with detailed information about caring for reptiles. Look for them at libraries, bookstores, and pet stores. These books will help you decide if you are ready to take care of a reptile.

Reptiles in Your Area

There are many ways to learn about wild reptiles in your area. Visit a local nature center where native reptiles are on display and talk to the naturalists who work there. If there isn't a nature center near by, contact your state wildlife agency. It might be called Department of Conservation, Department of Wildlife and Parks, or Department of Natural Resources.

These agencies can send you information about reptiles in your state.

Wonderful books called *Field Guides* can be checked out from libraries or purchased at bookstores. These books are used to identify reptiles and other creatures that live in the wild. *Field Guides* contain pictures, illustrations, and descriptions of animals living in different areas.

Sharing the World with Reptiles

Several species of reptiles are in danger of disappearing from our planet. Some of them are losing their homes due to habitat destruction. Others are hunted for their skins. Some people hurt reptiles simply because they are afraid of them.

You can help reptiles by learning more about them. You can study how they fit into their habitats. You can observe the beauty of their colors and patterns. You can discover the ways reptiles help us when they do their jobs in nature.

As you learn more about these remarkable creatures, please take the time to share with others what you have learned. The more people know how amazing reptiles are, the more they will appreciate them. When more people want to protect reptiles we can preserve their habitats, stop hunting them for their skins, and respect instead of fear them.

Please learn more about reptiles and the other animals that live in our world. Then share with others what you learn.

Glossary

caudal lure: Using a tail to attract a prey animal.

contaminated: When poisons or chemicals have polluted an area.

crocodilians: A group of reptiles that includes alligators, crocodiles, and gharials.

diurnal: An animal that is active during the day.

habitat: A place in nature where an animal lives.

heat pits: Sensors that allow some snakes to detect infrared heat.

herpetology: The study of reptiles and amphibians.

keratin: A protein that makes up hair, fingernails, and scales.

lamellae: Rows of microscopic hairs called setae that allow some lizards to stick to a surface.

nocturnal: An animal that is active at night.

omnivore: An animal that eats both plants and other animals.

predator: An animal that eats other animals.

prehensile tail: A tail that can grasp or hold like a toe or foot.

prey: An animal that is eaten by other animals.

rodents: A large group of mammals that includes animals such as mice, rats, squirrels, and beavers.

venomous reptile: A reptile with venom glands and the ability to inject the venom through biting.

Bibliography

- Adler, K. 1989. *Contributions to the History of Herpetology.* Society for the Study of Amphibians and Reptiles, Oxford, Ohio.

- Gotch, A. F. 1986. *Reptiles, Their Latin Names Explained.* Blansford Press Ltd., Poole, Great Britain.

- Groombridge, B. 1987. *The Distribution and Status of World Crocodilians, In Wildlife Management: Crocodiles and Alligators* (pp. 9-21). Edited by Grahame J.W. Webb, S. Charlie Manolis, and Peter J. Whitehead. Surrey Beatty & Sons Pty Limited, Chipping Norton, Australia.

- Henkel, F. W. and Schmidt, W. 1995. *Geckoes: Biology, Husbandry, and Reproduction.* Translated from the original German by John Hackworth. Krieger Publishing Company, Malabar, Florida.

- Mitchell, J. C. 1994. *The Reptiles of Virginia.* Smithsonian Institution Press, Washington, D.C.

- Ross, R.A. and Marzec, G. 1990. *The Reproductive Husbandry of Pythons and Boas.* The Institute for Herpetological Research, Stanford, California.

- Stafford, P. J. and Henderson, R. W. 1996. *Kaleidoscopic Tree Boas: The Genus Corallus of Tropical America.* Krieger Publishing Company, Malabar, Florida.

- Steineger, L. 1898. *The Poisonous Snakes of North America.* Smithsonian Institute Report. Facsimile Reproduction 1971. The Shorey Book Store, Seattle, Washington.

About the Author

Photo taken by Deana Mason

At the age of eight, David M. Nieves became captivated with reptiles while caring for a garter snake brought home by his brother. This began a lifelong fascination with the field of herpetology. He soon joined the junior naturalist program at the local nature center and, by the time he was in middle school, was sharing his knowledge of reptiles with elementary-school students in his hometown of Bellevue, Nebraska.

Since those early years, David has continued to devote himself to herpetology. He created Reptile Education and Research in 1990, a private facility dedicated to the study of reptiles and amphibians from around the world. Because of his strong commitment to educate others about this often misunderstood and feared group of animals, David speaks to thousands of people each year at schools, community centers, libraries, nature centers, and zoos. He is also busy working on more *Up Close* books. David lives near Bellevue, Nebraska with his wife, Michelle and their three daughters: Ciara, Savannah, and Mia.

Can you find the human skin?

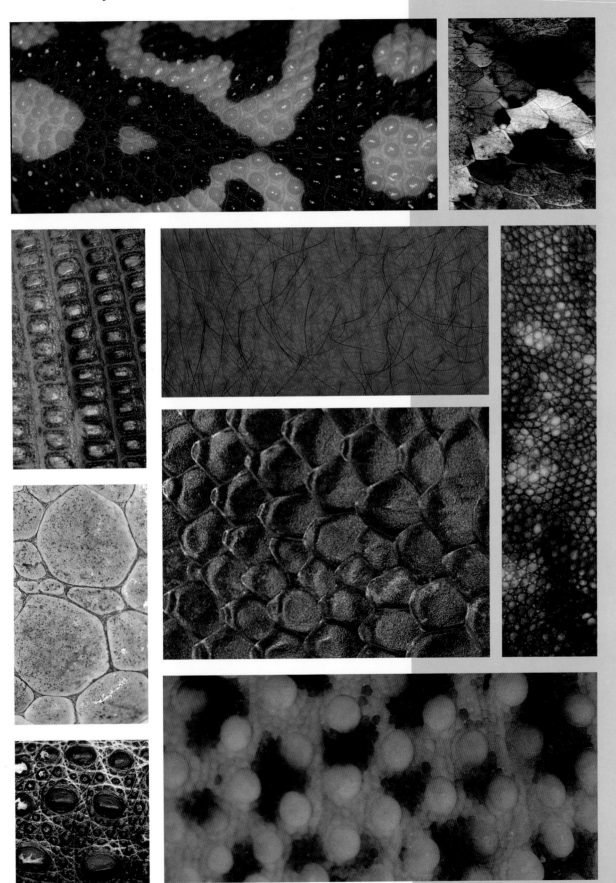

55

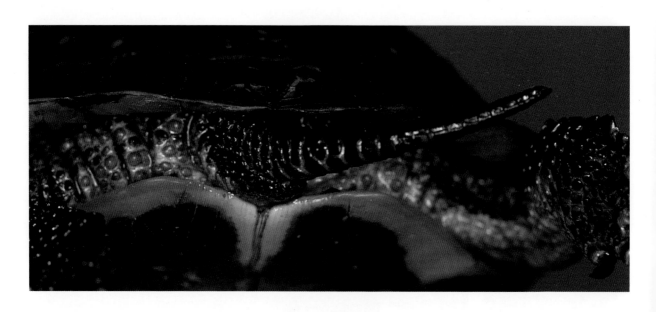

The End